In A Chicago Minute

by Mike Lubow

Published by Birdwatcher Books
Copyright © 2012 Mike Lubow
All rights reserved.
ISBN: 0615626815
ISBN-13: 978-0615626819

156
words

What's a Chicago minute?

You've probably heard the curious phrase, "In a New York minute." An old-time comic said it was the time between your light turning green and the guy behind you honking. Maybe New Yorkers do march to a faster drummer. But, our Chicago minutes march to a clock measured in words. No more than 160, ever. The pieces in this book all ran as columns in the Chicago Tribune on Sundays under the title "Got a Minute?" Whether they take you that long to read or not, they're Chicago-born, Chicago-bred, Chicago-styled. Their home town has been described by a poet as the "city of big shoulders." That's probably no more true than New York being a city of fast time. But, shoulders aside, Chicago has always been a city of big stories. This collection is an attempt to show that some of them can be expressed in the time it took you to read this.

Contents

159
words

Introduction

This'll only take a minute. Each of the following pieces contains no more than 160 words, a minute's worth. They show that brevity is still the soul of, well, if not wit, then of quirky insights. You develop an affinity for short stuff in an ad agency. When I was a writer there, my job was to create radio and TV scripts no longer than 60 seconds. But pushing soap, beer and fast food will only take a writer so far. Better subjects beckoned. Non-advertising minutes popped out of my keyboard. Sixty-second "un-ads." A Chicago Tribune editor was looking for a column that might appeal to readers' ever shortening attention spans. We talked, and my un-ads became a regular feature called "Got A Minute," running in the Sunday Tribune's Quality-of-Life "Q" section. Here they are again. Lightweight literary quickies to help clear the mind before you go on to something more hefty. Enjoy.

156
words

Malted Milk Balls

A father and son are on a city bench watching lunchtime crowds rush past. The boy has a box of malted milk balls and hands one to his dad. It accidentally drops and rolls down the sloping sidewalk toward the street. It gets about halfway before someone, unaware, crushes it underfoot. The father says, "Let's drop another, see how far it goes." Suddenly they've got a game. Taking turns, they let one malted milk ball at a time roll into the crowd of feet, rooting for theirs to go furthest. Some are squashed instantly; others go far. One or two make it all the way, untouched. A game of chance. Later the father remembers a TV program about people who lived to be 100. Some said they drank daily; some never drank. Some exercised; some didn't. Some were thin, some fat. Seems there was no secret. This makes the father think about the malted milk balls.

137
words

Banana

You're driving home on a clear night. Your wife's asleep and your little son's in the back, strapped in, jabbering to himself. You hear him say, "banana." It's one of his words. You've heard it at breakfast. Then he says it again, loudly so you'll pay attention. "Banana!" You figure the kid's hungry or just being silly. You shrug this off. Then you notice it. A big crescent moon hanging yellow and bright in the dark sky. It's unmistakable. A banana! Your son knows it's the moon. You guys always look at the moon together. Suddenly you realize that he's making an association. In his own simple way he's saying, "Dad, the moon looks like a banana!" And the kid's not even one year old. This guy's going to be smart. A lot smarter than you are.

140
words

Coffee

You're in the boardroom. Coffee cups and note pads litter the long table. Your new boss is sitting across from you, with no pad. He's so new he doesn't know he needs something to write on. This is your moment to win points, so you slide your pad toward him. It sails across the waxed surface with unanticipated force, knocking into his coffee cup, a perfect strike. The new boss is hopping in pain. Your corporate buddies are wide-eyed. To everyone, it looked like you plainly knocked this guy's coffee onto his lap for no reason. He eventually accepts your apologies although he always seems nervous around you after that. Inexplicably, this makes you popular with the other white-collar drones. Office life has always been a gold mine of comic moments, even before The Office became a hit TV show.

147
words

Genghis

You've seen the bumper-sticker wisdom, "He who dies with the most toys wins." Sorry, that's just corny, and it's about being dead, which is a downer. It should be, "He who dies with the most Y-chromosomes (male genetic markers) in future generations wins." This is a quick way of paying grudging respect to Genghis Khan, the rampaging Mongol who overran Eurasia in the 13th Century. He and his male heirs had a taste for harems and concubines. This may be distasteful by contemporary standards, but from a Darwinian standpoint, Genghis was the world's biggest father figure. According to Science magazine and genetic studies conducted at Oxford University, he had a reproductive rate estimated at 800,000 times the norm: 16 million guys carry Genghis' Y-chromosome today. That's 8 percent of all Eurasians; half a percent of all men on Earth. Genghis is long gone, but his line marches on.

143
words

Karate

When you see guys fight, it's utterly artless. Seems the more a guy knows about fighting the less likely he is to do it. There was a kid named Frankie who learned karate while in high school. He lived near a tough neighborhood and his dad wanted him to have the lessons. Frankie got one kind of colored belt after another. One day in the schoolyard, a skinny kid with a cigarette hanging from his lips bumped into Frankie. This kid was known for his mean disposition. Frankie stood his ground and the tough kid popped him bam, bam, too fast to see. Blood from Frankie's nose ran down his chin onto his clothes. The only color on Frankie's belt that day was red. Karate didn't help because it didn't make Frankie mean, and it didn't do anything about the other kid's meanness.

131
words

Holiday Car

A little boy sits in a kid-sized car that he got for the holidays. He's five. The car's made for sidewalks and playgrounds. Battery-powered, with knobby tires. You and the boy's parents, along with a few relatives hover around him in a party mood. You say things like, "Pretty cool, huh?" And, "Don't get any speeding tickets!" The boy sits, looking pensive. He's a thoughtful kid and his honesty about things is pure and unspoiled at five. After a pause, he looks up at the big people and says: "Do I know how to drive?" Some of the grown-ups laugh, but you know better. You know that this kid has just expressed the metaphoric question that every guy privately wrestles with—one way or another—for the rest of his life.

140
words

Warped

Two science books collide like peanut butter and chocolate. Just takes a minute to get a taste. In "Einstein" Walter Isaacson explains his hero's idea: everything depends on an observer's point of view. You think you're standing still, the other guy thinks you're moving. Typical Einstein. In "Before the Dawn," Nicolas Wade shows that humanity's warlike instincts come from our chimp ancestors who always saw the chimps in the next valley as evil. Doesn't matter which valley you're in. The chimps on the other side of the hill are the evil ones. Wade says our chimp DNA cannot be denied. Two books, one idea: Relativity. Einstein says you think you're standing still and the other guy's moving. Wade says that whichever group you're in, the other group is your enemy. Relativity explains that space is warped. Maybe war is, too.

135
words

Athletic Liars

Athletes used to be laughably bad actors when they did TV commercials. They'd say "thee best" instead of "the best" and "aye good cereal" instead of "a good cereal." You knew they were reading the words and you didn't mind their sounding unnatural; c'mon they're jocks. Now athletes are getting better at doing ads. They're too smooth, almost as good as pro actors. This is not cool. Athletes who appeared to struggle and bumble through ad copy sent us a subliminal message. (Subliminal advertising—powerful stuff.) The message was: "We don't really believe this garbage! We're being paid to say it. Nobody talks like this!" Today's athlete-actors don't send that message. By being good at performing ad copy they've just become good liars, and we understand that's their real message. The old message was a lot cooler.

146
words

The End of Nostalgia

Remember nostalgia? That bittersweet feeling you got when you heard an old song? Or saw a scene from an old TV show? Can't get that feeling any more. The old songs and TV shows are back. It's like they never left. You can find a radio station to tweak everyone's nostalgia. Hits of the '90s, '80s, '70s. Even golden oldies, for people who are, themselves, golden oldies. And these stations are popular with kids half your age. Same with vintage TV. Gleason's on. So is Twilight Zone, Brady Bunch, even a B&W Superman. If you enjoy these things again, nostalgia fades. The song that once brought memories of high school flooding back is the song you heard twenty times last month while driving to work. When you hear it now, it just reminds you of last month. The tweak is gone. Makes you nostalgic for nostalgia.

143

words

Dog Bar Scene

You're with your dog in the vet's crowded waiting room. And you get the quick impression of the bar scene in Star Wars. Remember? All those humanoids carousing. This came to mind because, for a minute, you imagine this room through your dog's eyes. Your Springer Spaniel sees a bug-eyed Boxer, then a Chow with its black tongue, a quivering little lap dog, a lumbering St. Bernard, drooling and panting. In a box on a lady's lap, there's a cat with wide yellow eyes. Your dog accepts this universe the way Obi Wan and Luke accepted happy-hour aliens as just fellow humanoids. You snap out of your dog's point of view and realize how uninteresting our world of people is. Dogs have canine-oids while we've got sameness. Any differences humans might have are trivial by comparison, if we even bother to notice them.

149
words

Big Guys

Big guys, say six-nine, 300 pounds, have an automatic advantage over the rest of us. We know this. They know it. Our women know it, too, which is somewhat embarrassing. Big guys can handle regular guys in a fight. Or stop a fight. You're out with your buddy, a gentle soul who's six-nine and a half. You get into a shoving match with some punk. You and the punk are five-ten, one eighty. You may or may not be good fighters. Doesn't matter. As soon as the shoving starts, your buddy strides over in his size fourteens and everyone knows the fight will never happen. It's the way of the world, the law of the jungle. Bigness rules. Size matters. Might makes right. We instinctively know this. Does this mean big guys are lucky they're big? Yeah, it does. And if we're friends with one, we're lucky, too.

141
words

Maine Sweatshirt

It's a wintry January weekend. You want to wear your warmest sweatshirt. The one with a hood and the word MAINE across the chest. Your wife got it from the university store there, knowing you're a fan of any place where there are moose. You can't find this shirt, and yell into the next room, "Honey, where's my MAINE sweatshirt!" She doesn't hear you, so you try again, louder, as you walk through the house. "Anybody seen my MAINE sweatshirt?" Your kid comes up and asks, "Dad, don't you have, like, a second choice?" You answer that you really want your MAINE sweatshirt. You can't understand the funny look he gives. A minute later you race after him to explain, but he's out for the day, probably telling his friends that his dad had a main sweatshirt and couldn't find it.

143
words

Too Much Choice

You're in a big bookstore. There are tens of
thousands of books. Tables of best sellers, racks
of magazines. And around the bend, more books.
You're sure to find one you want, right? But you
don't; nothing turned you on. A week later you're
in a Florida hotel. You go into the little shop where
there's a motley collection of candy, bug spray,
T-shirts and a rack with maybe ten paperback
books. You happily buy the least bad one and take
it to the pool. Turns out, it's a fun read. But you'd
never have chosen it from the huge collection in the
big store back home. Part of the pleasure comes
from having less to cram through your decision-
making machinery. Once again, architect Mies van
der Rohe's "less is more" advice comes to mind. Or
should it be "fewer" is more?

149
words

Holiday Bazaar

Tis the season for "heartwarming" stories. Like the family battling four kinds of diseases but their neighbors bring gifts. Anybody really want to read this stuff? Instead of reflecting upon the goodness of mankind, you're horrified by the description of disease. Here's something better, perhaps: You're a tourist exploring a middle-eastern marketplace. You've been warned against wandering alone because thieves, pickpockets and unscrupulous merchants are said to be real dangers. Still, you risk it. You buy some postcards, pay quick and get out of the shop alive. A block away, you notice a bearded man in robes pushing through the crowd, yelling at you! You freeze. He approaches, bows, then in heavily accented English he says, "Sir, you forgot your change." He hands you a few coins. You don't care about this change, but it does change your mind about people, and your heart's warmed a bit. Peace.

141
words

Sourdough Minute

One of the best things about sitting down to a good meal is the immediate pleasure of bread or rolls. You're hungry, and there's no waiting. But sometimes you find yourself taking a big bite of sourdough. It looks like the normal white bread you expect. But it doesn't have the pure, bready taste. It tastes—sour. C'mon. When milk turns sour, we throw it out. Sourdough contains bacteria (also known as "germs") that create tangy lactic acid. Sourdough bakers carefully protect their specific bacterium, and save a little raw dough from each batch as "starter" to add its distinctive flavor to the next. Sure, this is all a matter of personal taste. If you like sour bread, go for it. But it's just wrong to assume that everyone does. Such an assumption can get the meal off on a sour note.

149
words

Loyal Dog

This minute is for dogs who sit in kennels waiting for you to return from vacation. Even if the kennel is a "pet hotel" that serves frozen yogurt, your dog must wonder, what happened to the world? In other words, what happened to you? Remember the Scottish terrier named Bobby who made a name for himself in Edinburgh? He accompanied night watchman John Gray for years. They were inseparable. When John died, Bobby went to the grave and stayed through all weather, surviving by the kindness of townspeople who occasionally brought food. This happened in the 1870s, and as Europeans will do, they built a statue honoring the little dog. But dogs don't care about statues. They care about you. Something to think about when you're vacationing and your dog's waiting. How long did Bobby stay by his master's grave? Until his own death, 14 years later.

154
words

Malleable Minutes

The minute is a malleable thing. Malleable is a word
most of us don't know. That's okay because most
of us don't know the true nature of the minute.
Malleable means changeable, moldable. Minutes
are not rigid chunks of time. There are morning
minutes and evening minutes, two vastly different
things. You wake up in the morning and look at
your bedside clock. It reads 6:30. You daydream
for a while, then look at the clock and it's 7:15. You
weren't sleeping, but 45 minutes have passed. Now
imagine that it's 6:30 in the evening. You're watching
a TV show, say Seinfeld. You watch TV until halfway
through the next show, say According To Jim. Now
it's 7:15. Same amount of minutes have passed. But
it feels much longer than it did when you were lying
in bed. Morning minutes. Evening minutes. Vastly
different things. The malleable minute. And you just
spent one here.

153
words

Ball Throw

Sometimes it takes just a minute to redefine yourself to yourself. Example: High school gym. The coach is putting you through outdoor fitness evaluations. One is the "ball throw." Each guy throws a softball and someone measures the distance. You figure you'll get an average score; you're a pretty average guy. The class jocks whipped the ball 50, 60 yards. You have no expectations, but you give it a fling. Amazingly, your throw soars into a high arc and when it passes the point where the farthest shots have hit, it's still rising. Your ball lands so far away that the kid with the measuring tape just gapes. The coach gapes. You feel fine, but you're surprised that you had such a throw in you. Gives you something good to think back on as you go through life. Must be the way a detective feels, knowing he's packing a gun under his jacket.

149
words

Email

Words derived from e-mail have created an e-reverent "e-jargon." There's edress (your e-mail address), etail (e-shopping), evisionism (rewriting history via the net), and emailingering (wasting time by emailing). To say nothing about "emoticons," keyboard symbols that convey smiles, frowns, winks and even a tongue sticking out (:-P). Now there's egnore, which is what you do to an e-mail you don't want to answer. It's like letting your voicemail take calls when you don't want a 2-way talk. E-mail offers maximum conversation control. You can send and read with no obligation to respond. You're free, "e-free." The world-shattering equation, "E=mc2" can be evised to "E=mc/2." Or, "E-mail equals My Conversation divided by 2" which means it's only "My Conversation." Trouble is, in a communications system that allows you to egnore, you can be egnored, yourself. And if you use those hokey emoticons, maybe you should be.

151
words

Skip

Your heart skipped a beat. What was that about?
Felt like a fish jumping. Your doctor says, yeah, it
happens. He does some tests to be sure all is fine.
You could be any age, he says, most guys don't even
notice these "extra beats." But your mind drifts to
the memory of tragic athletes whose hearts ran
out of synch. You worry, but soon forget about it.
Then you see an adventure film about a bush pilot
in Alaska. Over the mountain wilderness his plane's
engine sputters, coughs, misfires. Man, this could
be trouble. But in a minute the engine recovers,
smoothes out, and all is fine. Suddenly, you see a
connection. A single-engine plane has no backup.
And you realize, that's you. That's each of us. We're
all single-engine airplanes. This disturbing thought
makes your pulse race for a minute, and you just
hope it doesn't skip a beat.

153
words

Old Guys

From a distance, he looks like a guy you know
from the neighborhood. Baseball cap, team jacket,
faded jeans and running shoes. Then you get up
close, and—what? That's no guy, that's somebody's
kindly old grandpa. Could be your long-retired high
school principal. Or ancient Mr. Burns from The
Simpsons. Wrinkles, age spots, multiple chins, silver
sideburns. Old guys don't dress like old guys any
more. They used to wear what Humphrey Bogart
wore in black and white films. And they used to
wear flat caps. Those caps, which shouted "old
guy," must have been issued to every man before
he could collect social security. That was then. Now,
it's baseball caps and clothes from the mall. You can
only discover that the guy's not a kid by looking
at his face. Then he looks back at you with an
expression that says, "what're you lookin' at?" And
you gotta admit: good question.

156
words

Teddy

They don't make guys like him any more. 55, overweight and retired after a long career. But there he was, on a jaguar hunt in the wildest part of the Amazon jungle. Left camp with a party of native Brazilian guides. He didn't return on time, and his friends got worried. Then one of the Brazilians came into camp and collapsed. Later that day another guide staggered in, too tired to speak. No sign of our guy. His buddies organized a rescue party and went looking. Soon they came across yet another Brazilian guide lying half-dead on the crude trail. They helped him to camp, and continued into the jungle. Finally they saw their friend. He was carrying one of the remaining guides, bringing this much younger man to safety. When asked how he was feeling, our guy said, "I'm bully!", his version of "fine." They talked that way back in 1913. Especially this guy, Teddy Roosevelt.

153
words

Life Lottery

Watching the lottery drawing can waste a minute, especially if you haven't bought a ticket. But there's something symbolic in it, a cruel commentary about our personal chances for success. It's all in the randomly bouncing balls. One pops out with its lucky number. It's no better than any of the other balls, but there it is, a winner. Consider this: our chance of succeeding at something works the same way! Imagine a bunch of us with equal talent, whether it's for basketball, rock guitar, telling jokes, whatever. We're like those ping-pong balls, each with a shot at breaking out. But only some do it. Purely by chance. Makes you wonder how many OTHER Michael Jordans, Paul McCartneys or Jay Lenos, have been out in the world, bouncing around, and nobody ever knew. How many are out there right now who we'll never know? The lottery's not just a money game. It's life.

150
words

Pill Minute

Maybe it's a cousin or an office buddy. Someone you've known for a while. And suddenly, the guy is nicer, unnaturally friendly. He's even showing a sensitive side you didn't know existed. All because of anti-depressants. These pills are becoming almost as common as aspirin and antacids. Doctors even prescribe them to help ex-smokers deal with nicotine withdrawal. But what happened to the cave man you've known and liked? You have to wonder: who is the real him? This sweet guy? Or the pre-pill grouchy guy? If these pills can remake your personality, how can you know the real person in you? Maybe there isn't a real you. Maybe you're just a chemical robot, and your mind is some kind of appliance that can be tuned like a radio. That's a pretty disturbing thought. Even a depressing one. But if becomes too depressing, don't worry. There's a pill for that.

153
words

Clinton Gift

Maybe you got Bill Clinton's fat autobiography for the
holidays. It's a good guy gift. Clinton makes a good
guy story. Should take more than a minute to size up
an ex-president, but here's goes: Clinton played every
card in the deck. That's why he had an interesting
life and ran the free world for two terms. "Every card
in the deck" means he made every person available
to him. He had absolutely no prejudice. Not even
the benign, unspoken kind. He embraced (don't say
it) everyone. Minorities, non-minorities, foreigners,
young, old, the disabled, the curiosities and the
geniuses. Clinton's best friend was an African-
American guy. A beloved father figure was that Israeli
leader who got shot. Some public figures talk the talk
about a rainbow of people, but Clinton really saw it,
and understood its value. He might not have been
the best American president, but he was the most
American president.

157

words

Art Class

Visiting an art museum dredges up a memory:
College days. Art class had no appeal, so you didn't
sign up. The teacher was known to cry "let yourself
be free!" Not your kind of guy. Then you heard they
were doing figure drawing, nude models. To a lonely
freshman, this was big. So one day you sneak into
the art room, hiding among the legitimate students,
a daring, stunt. And you start sketching. The model's
fat, something you didn't expect. But she's definitely
nude, so you're not complaining. Having no talent,
you draw her as a blob of overlapping circles. Circle
body, circle head, circles for, well, everything. It's
cartoonish, but you're an imposter so who cares.
Then the teacher points to you and bellows "Hey!"
You figure you're busted. But the guy grabs your
sketch and waves it around saying, "This is what I'm
talking about, people, what freedom!" He moves on,
giving you a smile.

155
words

Man of Few Words

A man of few words, now he's an easy guy to like.
You don't run into his kind often. That's why you
oughta get the novel "No Country For Old Men."
It's by Cormac McCarthy, a terse coot once known
to hang out in an El Paso poolroom. Don't worry,
this isn't a book review. We're on the Guy Page,
with limited space. That's OK; we're talking about a
guy book, and we don't need more room. McCarthy
writes in Texan. Not presidential Texan, ranger
Texan. Hemingway tried this but never got the
squint right. Larry McMurtry's "Lonesome Dove"
came close. Then he wrote about women with
soap opera-type problems, and you gotta wonder
where he's coming from. Enough talk. Read "No
Country…" It's got too much violence, but not
as much as the news. That's not what it's about
anyway. It's about language, the language of Texan,
a language of few words, guy language.

151
words

Piña Colada

A tropical drink is not a guy drink. It comes in a fancy glass or maybe in a coconut. There's a showy wedge of pineapple sticking out, with a cherry on top. And a little purple paper umbrella. Not guy things. One problem: The drink can taste good. A mix of tropical fruits frozen like a milk shake, and laced with rum. These flavors suggest hula dancers, steel drums, escape. You can even get 151 proof rum that will knock you on your butt. But still, you feel uncomfortable holding the gimmicky glass, sipping from it; you can't order it. So you get a beer, and let the ladies have their tropical drinks, along with any guys who don't mind the pineapple and cherry image. You laugh at how foolish these drinkers look as they twirl their little umbrellas. They might not hear you laughing, though. Not over their own laughter.

154
words

Toad Guy

A bunch of guys are at a picnic in the forest preserve. Drinking, shooting the bull, being guys. One sees a toad. "Yo, a toad. Let's grab it." They kneel over this warty creature who looks at them with prehistoric contempt. The toad knows he can jump if they get too close. One guy reaches. Toad jumps. This sudden movement tweaks an inborn danger response and the guy recoils like a baby. Then one guy pushes forward and scoops up the toad before it can even think of jumping again. The toad is surprised by this scoop because it came with no hesitation. Now the toad's cupped in two strong hands, being stroked and studied. The toad's not the only one who's surprised. The other guys are, too, because the toad's picker-upper was a young woman. A skinny, pretty blonde. Once again, we reluctantly have to admit: sometimes a girl can be a guy.

156
words

Tastes Like Chicken

When adventurous eaters, travelers to exotic lands,
explorers of strange menus, describe unusual meat
they invariably say "It tastes like chicken." We've
heard this so often, it's a tired joke. Rattlesnake?
Alligator? "Tastes like chicken." Possum, rabbit?
"Just like chicken." Distasteful as it may seem to
us, dog and cat, which in some cultures are just
another kind of meat, have been described as, again,
chicken. Enough. But then you're innocently eating
some kind of spicy chicken dish in a restaurant
specializing in a regional cuisine that we won't
mention because all regional cuisine the same
basic adventure anyway. This chicken dish contains
tender, light and dark chunks, a neutral, pleasant-
tasting meat flavored with strong spices. Suddenly
the thought hits you: the old phrase, "It tastes like
chicken," can WORK BOTH WAYS. What if an
unscrupulous or budget-conscious chef put chopped
squirrel in the stew. It would taste like…yeah! And
you'd never know, would you?

153
words

Three-time Rule

Some guys live by a strong, silent rule that goes "never apologize, never explain." This rule has been attributed to Immanuel Kant, or maybe it was John Wayne. Who cares who first said it. If we get it wrong, we don't have to apologize. Or explain. Today, we introduce a new guy philosophy cut from the same cloth. A philosophy that reflects a guy's independent spirit. Here goes: "Never ask a third time." Just as you feel diminished by apologizing or explaining, you also diminish yourself by violating this third-time rule. Whether you're applying for a job, asking for a raise, a date, a favor, an answer to a question, or you just want the salt. You ask once and get nowhere, okay. Ask again, and it's a reminder. If you still strike out, forget it. The term strike out is right on. We know how the words, "strike three" make us feel.

154
words

Age Inflation

Old guys say, "time speeds up when you're my age."
We're tired of hearing this. But what if they're right?
Is there an inflation factor affecting years, as it does
dollars? We see magazine articles that say "40 is the
new 30," and "50 is the new 40." Can this be true?
Is 60 the new 50? Is 100 the new 90? That's what
would happen if years, like dollars, bought less. But
instead of buying less stuff, they buy less time. So
even though you've got 30 hard-won years to your
name, in today's market they're only worth, say, 20.
You get the respect of a 20-year old and probably
dress like one. Maybe the Fed's inflation expert
Alan Greenspan could be consulted. Not that a
70-something can be entirely trusted to tell us how
the passage of time feels. But these days, he's one of
the new 60-somethings, and that could help.

152
words

Baseball Hit

A real guy doesn't wince, say ouch, jump around in pain and rub a booboo. But, it's hard to keep your cool when a rock-hard baseball thrown by a rock-hard major league pitcher slams into your ribs at 90 miles an hour. Or maybe the ball hits your elbow, hip or thigh. Hits with a force that can chip bone, bruise muscle, bust veins and cause a black-and-blue mark that'll last a month. This kind of body shot can create a sudden shock of pain that makes a guy want to scream like a little girl. But what do big league hitters do when this happens? Mostly, they just glower at the pitcher for a moment, then jog to first with dignity. And they DON'T TOUCH the spot that got hit. They don't acknowledge it. Not touching the sore spot is the ultimate guy rule here. And these are the ultimate guys.

156
words

Steaks

You're in this fancy steak house, and you're not hungry. You had a big lunch earlier in the day. But it's your anniversary, so you're taking your wife out for a nice meal, as planned. Not only are you not hungry, but the price of steaks is out of sight. Your wife says, "Oh, look honey, you don't have to get a large one, they have small ones." She's right. The menu lists a 16-ounce filet or sirloin and an 8-ounce version of each. When the waiter takes your order, it's no contest. You order the 16-ouncer, the largest steak possible. It costs way too much and you don't want all that meat. But you know that a guy can't order a small steak, which is described as the petite cut. Your wife doesn't understand. She thinks you're nuts. That may be true, but your hands are tied. Come on, they called it the petite cut!

158
words

Two Guys

There are two kinds of guys. One is sure. The other isn't. Let's call the first guy "declarative guy." He declares that, say, the Dow will hit 11,000 this year. No discussion. This guy holds court when he talks, and doesn't entertain objections. He ought to have said: MAYBE the Dow will hit 11,000. That's what the other guy would say. Call this other guy "maybe guy." To him, everything is opinion. "Maybe guy" is easier to take. And he's correct. Quantum theory proves the universe is a giant "maybe." Subatomic particles, the stuff of everything, behave unpredictably. Physicists have to say: MAYBE a particle will go straight, not IT WILL. Are you "declarative guy" or "maybe guy?" The only time it's good to be declarative is if you're a doctor. (Nobody wants to hear, "Maybe you're okay." We want, "You ARE okay.") In other situations, "maybe guy" rules. After all, he's right about everything in the universe.

159
words

Ready

You're waiting for your wife. She said she'll be down in a minute. You're dressed and on schedule, the schedule she set. You're going to her friend's party and she doesn't want to be late. Since she'll be a minute you figure you'll spend the time writing a minute's worth of stuff while you wait. You'll write about how you're glad you're out of the immediate dressing area, because you know about the "brown dress or green dress" question which has no right answer. Or about the "does this make me look..." question. Just 'cause it's common doesn't make it any less dangerous. You've only got a minute, and you'll be on your way. This bit of writing should be just the right length, because you only want to write for a minute. But wait. You're still writing. Writing more than a minute's worth. This has to stop. You turn on the ball game, and put your feet up.

157

words

Memorial Day

Memorial Day! Is this a serious holiday or another excuse for a 3-day weekend? There's no way we want to make it into something serious. Seriousness goes against the holiday mood, right? This is a chance to picnic and have a beer. Get outdoors, cook hot dogs, goof around. Or watch Indy on TV with the remote on your belly and not think seriously about anything. No work Monday. Life is good. Then you find yourself stopping, beer in hand. And before you drink, you pause. This is a private thing. Nobody sees you do it. You wink, you give a quick nod. Then you drink. You do these invisible little gestures as a kind of toast. You can't help it. You remember guys who were soldiers, guys who ARE soldiers, guys who came back and who didn't. They're worth tipping a beer to, right? So you do. Not that you're getting serious. C'mon, it's a holiday.

160
words

Popcorn

You've got a minute 'til the movie starts. One guy
ahead of you in the popcorn line. Plenty of time.
Then he orders nachos. With cheese, which has
to be spooned on. And chilies. The counter girl
is suddenly a short order cook, a job she's not
qualified for. She's qualified for putting popcorn in
bags. Okay, she's back. He asks for a cardboard
tray, and you realize he's getting stuff for friends.
Now he orders a hot dog. And a baked pretzel which
belongs in a beer hall, not a movie theater. Popcorn
belongs in a movie theater. Popcorn! The hot dog's
supposed to slide into a tight, silver bag, and the
girl's having trouble fitting it in. Seconds tick,
precious seconds as your movie starts. The pretzel
is being microwaved. Then the guy orders a cherry
slushy! Forget it. You go watch your movie with no
popcorn, which you should've had in a minute. But
the minute's up.

158
words

Globalism

There's a new book by Thomas Friedman
called "The World is Flat." In 488 pages, it
discusses globalism. Globalism is the end of
regional differences, a way of describing today's
interconnectedness of nations, businesses,
individuals, blah, blah. Here's a faster insight into
this phenomenon. You're at a pub in rural Ireland.
It's in a small village on the rugged western coast,
near nothing but sheep and isolated mountains.
Your waitress is a milk-fed Irish country girl. Fair
and freckled, wearing a tiny cross, speaking with a
Gaelic lilt. You figure there's not much in the way of
international pop culture in her world. But when she
turns away from your table, her shirt rides up a little
and you can't help but notice a tattoo on her lower
back. One of those curly designs that American girls
have. And English girls. And Japanese girls. You
just got a glimpse of globalism, without reading any
book about it.

158
words

Skunk

One minute you're walking your dog and everything's cool in the night-time park. A minute later you're in a world of stink. Your dog flushed a skunk that went into battle mode. Butt first and tail up, it sprays a scent from chemical hell into your dog's face. But that's not the worst of it. Your dog LIKES it. This dog, who will now smell skunky for a year, LIKES it. No flinching, no backing away. Instead, she gets this "I'm in heaven" look, inhaling deeply, eyes half-shut. The mutt's in ecstasy. And you've got to wonder—since a dog's nose is more than 40 times more sensitive than ours, why do dogs dig bad smells? They roll in dead squirrels and goose droppings. They wear odors proudly like medals. You don't have to travel to jungles, look under the sea, or even go to other planets to find the weird. It's sleeping at the foot of your bed.

157
words

King of Queens

The ultimate guy sitcom is the oddly named "King of Queens." Kevin James plays a deliveryman who loves junk food, junk TV and gets yelled at a lot. He is you! Problem is, the name of the show. Okay, Queens is a borough of New York and the guy lives there. But the pun doesn't work. He's no king; his wife dominates him. And if you didn't know Queens is a place, you might think he's a king of queens, whatever that means. Try "king of guys," maybe. But, like we said, he's not the king type. This is a modern "Honeymooners." That classic 1950's show wasn't well named, either. "Honeymooner" Jackie Gleason and his wife were in their 40s, married for years! Just forget names. If you haven't seen King of Queens because you thought it was about a king or queens or whatever, watch it. Call it the Kevin James show. That name makes sense.

157
words

Premature Handshake

Of all the tricks guys use to establish dominance,
the premature handshake is one of the worst.
(Or best, if you're the aggressor.) It happens fast.
Two guys reach out to shake. This should mean
fingers wrap equally around each hand, and both
guys squeeze. Assuming one doesn't out-squeeze
the other, a stunt that could backfire, the shake's
okay. But if one guy wants to one-up the other, he
goes in for the premature shake. He clamps down
early, before the two hands completely interlock,
grabbing the victim's four outstretched fingers
in mid-knuckle. The loser can only squeeze back
half-heartedly, feeling like a wuss. He's lost face,
lost pride, lost dominance, lost the contest. All
he can do is wait 'til next time. As the unknown
philosopher said, sometimes you eat the bear,
sometimes the bear eats you. You lost that shake,
but maybe you'll get the next one. We're never far
from the cave, you know?

159
words

Blink

The popular book "Blink. The Power of Thinking Without Thinking," by Malcolm Gladwell, confirms our gut feelings. We don't need long, tedious experience to know something. Quick example: Students were asked to rate the quality of certain college teachers by looking at a 30-second videotape of the teachers' lecturing. After a semester of classes with these same teachers, the students rated them again and the ratings were identical. So the researchers pushed the envelope. With another group of students, they shortened the pre-semester video to TWO SECONDS. These students made their ratings. At semester's end, follow-up ratings matched the 2-second impressions with an accuracy of 95%! So know this: When you take an hour-long job interview, you and your would-be boss have probably sized up each other—correctly—in the first moment. Gladwell's book quickly confirms that we get things quickly. Wonder why he needed a whole book to make the point. We did it here in a minute.

153
words

Super Bowl

Let's take a minute to say something about the Super Bowl that should have been said long ago. Lose the X's and I's! Is this algebra or football? How many of us can read these Roman numerals? And even if we can, what do they have to do with the game? It's true that X's and O's have an honorable role in chalkboard diagrams. But not X's and I's, to say nothing about V's, etc. Who wants to decipher "Super Bowl XXXIX?" This ancient numbering system has been made obsolete by the invention of honest numbers we can understand, as in "Super Bowl 39." Let's use them. Come on, football commissioner, make this the last year that the big game is saddled with unnecessary, show-offy, incomprehensible Roman numerals. It's got to stop eventually, because you sure don't want to call it "Super Bowl L" in eleven years, do you? So stop it now.

154
words

"Mynoot"

The word "minute" is good. It's the basis for this Guy Page bit that occasionally appears. We know what this word means. As in "got a minute." Or, "I'll only be a minute." But this word, spelled the same way, is sometimes pronounced "my-noot." This is not a good word. It's an affected word, meaning "small." If we wanted to avoid simply saying small when we mean small, we could use other words like tiny, little, not-so-big and even diminutive. (Ah, there's a hint of "my-noot" in that last one, sneaky but not as bothersome), or a bunch of other synonyms without resorting to the foppish "my-noot." This word is confusing. When written, it looks like "minute" and it could take a guy a minute to figure out whether it means minute, or my-noot, by analyzing context, and do you need that aggravation? You don't have more than a minute to spend reading things anyway.

160
words

Slime

Maybe some of us like snails. Okay. But let's take a minute to look at what we're eating. We have melted butter. Garlic. And a powerful marketing idea, which we'll mention in a minute. This combination of mouth-feel and marketing can get an otherwise discerning guy to eat snails in our better restaurants against our better judgment. See, a snail is a mucus worm. A flatworm, a slug with a shell attached. It moves by sliding on a layer of mucus that it SECRETES. This mucus must come from inside its body, right? So when we eat snails, we're eating their little mucus-making organs, along with spare mucus, right? Why would we do such an unfathomable thing? The ingenious marketing idea, that's why! It's this: They're called "Escargots." This fancy foreign name gives them a mystique akin to the mystique enjoyed by foreign films, which can also be a hard to fathom. Maybe we need subtitles with our gourmet pretensions.

159
words

Bright Season

You're sitting in your favorite bar, nursing a post-holiday beer in peace. No need to apologize for this indulgence during our wholesome holiday season. Santa knows you're entitled to the moment. You're no stranger to this place, or this beer. Both are old friends. But why does the bar feel...nicer? And it hits you. The lights. Your bar, friendly neighborhood home away from home, is lit up with little holiday lights. They're strung across the ceiling, over the bottles, around doors and windows. Christmas was over yesterday, but these lights are still doing their thing. You hate to say it—it's not your style to talk this way–but they're kind of pretty. They give the place a...glow. Normally, you don't care about things in a bar being pretty—except for tall, blond Donna who tends there mid-week. No, you don't care that they're pretty. But you gotta wonder, why don't they have these little lights all year 'round?

160
words

Two Kinds of Jobs

There are two kinds of jobs. The kind you know
how to do and the kind you don't. Take a minute to
consider this. Say, for example, you drive the rental
car shuttle at the airport. You know how to do this
job. Circle around, pick up, drop off, take breaks,
wear the uniform, punch out, same thing again
tomorrow. Nice. Now, instead, imagine you have
to face something unfamiliar every day. Something
you haven't seen before. You have to dream up a
slogan nobody ever thought of, invent a new legal
strategy, diagnose a tricky disease. You don't know
how you're going to do it, exactly, or even if you
can. The first kind of job means little stress, little
bucks. Fair enough. The second means more stress,
more money. Which do you want? Mastery of the
familiar? Or wrestling with the uncertain? This is
the essential guy question. And, you know, it might
just be a toss up.

160
words

Father-son

Father-son relationships take more than a minute
to cover. But they can change in a minute. Like this:
You've got your first job. Wearing a tie, making your
own way. Except your dad picks you up at quitting
time because it's on his way home. On this day,
your company gave you a flyer about a father-son
softball game they're having. Absently, you toss it
on the car seat. Your eye is on the girls waiting at
the company's bus stop. Your dad sees the flyer. He
says, "Father-son game? Ah, too bad, I gotta work
Saturday." You didn't want to go anyway. Suddenly,
you both realize the game is for fathers at your
company and THEIR sons. The days of you and your
dad going to such things are over. Your dad realizes
this instantly, too, and there's a minute of discomfort
while you both laugh off his mistake. Soon, you start
taking the bus, talking to those girls.

156
words

Arthouse

You're sitting in an art house cinema watching a foreign film. Subtitles. Angst. Boredom. And you wonder, simply, why are you there? You know the answer, but we'll get to that in a minute. Here's a little game to play, a mental game you can try while attending any foreign film, dance recital or stage show where, say, bald guys with painted heads are doing mime stuff. Look around at the audience. Now imagine that the women aren't there. Their seats are suddenly empty. (This is a Twilight Zone thing–just go with it.) So now there are only guys. Guys without dates. They look around, blinking, confused. Slowly, they start to leave, ignoring the show. Then in great numbers they stand up and head for the exits. It hits you: Guys would never have been there without women. But we DO go to these things. What does this mean? We love our women, that's all.

153
words

Hand Print

You call that art? What else can you say when you see a hand print on a cave wall. You're in the Southwest, but it doesn't matter. Such hands are on cave walls in France, Australia, many places. Prehistoric man had a thing about hand prints. The scientists who comment on this stuff call it "cave art." But is it art? Art's supposed to reach out and touch your imagination. When the prehistoric painter leaves us a buffalo hunt or buxom maiden, well, maybe. Yet along with these you still get that smeared hand, fingers splayed above a blotchy palm. But wait: when you think about it, it's okay. There was a guy who said "I was here." Now he's long dead and you're thinking about him. You're thinking about him right now, that long-dead dude with the smeared hand. He's touched your imagination 40,000 years later. Maybe it is art, after all.

155
words

No Idea

You've got one minute to think of an idea.
Everybody's looking at you. You're in this new
job. A "creative" job. Something that doesn't get
your hands dirty. Something a real guy might
scoff at. A white wine job. Not a draft beer job (and
this bothers you). You're in your first brainstorm
meeting. Brainstorm is an unpleasant word; as a kid
you thought it was a disease. Such neurotic musings
mean you belong with the kindred spirits in this
conference room filled with other neurotics wearing
orange ties, frayed jeans, hair that's too long or too
short, the creative staff. Your boss says, gimme an
idea! The clock's ticking. You freeze. He looks at
you with corporate fury. He says, I need ideas, not
silence. And you think—how am I going to do this?
How am I going to work at this for the next 30 or 40
years? You have no idea.

160
words

Blue Collar

Comic Jeff Foxworthy has a show on the WB network (not Fox) called Blue Collar TV. It's about the redneck types that he's built his act around, and it's pretty funny. One problem: The show's name. Too limiting! By calling itself Blue Collar TV, it makes white collar guys and no collar guys feel left out. Truth is, most guys like beer cans, built blondes, pizza-littered rooms, raunchy humor, and the feel of a jukebox bar. The Guy Page recommends that Blue Collar TV should be called, simply, Guy TV. If they called it that, they'd get more viewers and this could help them stay on the air, which they might not do as far as we know. TV shows have the life spans of flies. In fact, by the time this minute's over, Blue Collar TV may have gone beer belly up. But the Man Show wasn't as funny and it had a four-year run on the Comedy channel.

157
words

Football Minute

There was a great football movie called "The Longest Yard," but there ought to be a movie called "The Longest Minute." A yard's always 3 feet, but a football minute's flexible. Picture this. You're watching the end of the Bears game, and your wife is waiting so you can go visit relatives. You truthfully say, "Only a minute to play." She figures, OK. Then there's a timeout. Then a penalty. A sideline pass stops the clock. Seven and a half minutes in real time have passed. The QB runs out of bounds. Then an injury stops the clock. There's a commercial. Two minutes, maybe three of beer and cars. We're back. Madden says, "Forty-three seconds, and the Bears are threatening." What's really threatening is your wife, glaring at you with her coat on. It's been like 10 minutes now, this football minute, and who knows how much longer the game will go? Ah, the flexible football minute.

160
words

Bees

You're in Italy, on a cliff overlooking the sea. The place is serene, like an oil painting. And it could be spoiled in the time it takes to read this. Just watch: It's an old monastery, something the guidebook recommended. You were dubious. But when you got there, it really was like a painting, and you were in it. Olive trees. A whitewashed building in sunshine. Rows of flowers. The humming of bees. An old lady in a black shawl sits in an ancient rocking chair, an essential part of the art. You're alone. For a minute, it's quiet–except for the bees. Then, comes a tour bus with air brakes and tourists. Tourists, suddenly everywhere. Taking pictures of each other, blocking out the sea, destroying the quiet. The lady in black is gone. You wonder, was she ever there? And you notice that you don't hear the bees. You hear people laughing, but they'll never know about the bees.

159
words

Speedy

There's this sexy, retro sitcom playing, and you've got nothing better to watch. The teen guy says to his red-haired girlfriend that he doesn't have a lot of time to make love, since his parents will be home soon. "But," he says, "all I need is a minute." Canned laughs. She says, smirking, "I know!" More canned laughs. This is, of course, a put-down. But you've got to wonder: why? Guys like things fast. Cars, motorcycles, food. And guys like sex. So what's so terrible about fast sex? Our females ought to be pleased we're so excited by them that we're speedy. And let's keep things in perspective. The African lion takes about 30 seconds. The bonobo chimpanzee, our close relative, is done in 13 seconds. Turtles take a little more time, but hey, they're turtles. By animal kingdom standards, a minute's not bad. It's the amount of time it took to read this. And could've been better spent.

160
words

Greed

After a minute of watching the reality show Survivor
or its urban spin-off, the Apprentice (possible
alternate title: Toadies in Training), you might
be reminded of the grand fun perpetrated on the
greedy by Mr. Guy Grand, "the grand guy." He was
a character in Terry Southern's 1960 satiric novel,
The Magic Christian. Grand erected a vat of manure
in Chicago's Loop, then sprinkled in thousand-
dollar bills. He even heated the cesspool, saying "…
that'll make it hot for them." He stood by while no
end of willing money grubbers grubbed through
the reeking swill, undergoing no end of indignity
to possibly clasp some free money in their paws.
Could this be what's meant by gross income? The
so called Survivors and the servile Apprentices of
today's TV game shows are jumping through hoops
of humiliation every week, proving that Terry
Southern's cynical views of human folly are as
crudely on target today as ever, if not more so.
More next time.

158
words

July 4th

It's America's birthday and there's the impulse to
take a minute and think about something American.
But let's not go over the tired territory of founding
fathers and fireworks. See how this works: You're
in an Asian restaurant on Hollywood's Sunset
Strip. You've come to California to make a TV
commercial. What's more American than TV
commercials? And this cute Japanese waitress
comes over, bowing cutely, and in halting English
she tries to take your order. But there's a language
gap. Your business buddy asks her how long she's
been here. Not long, she says, and explains that
she's a student at UCLA, majoring in Spanish,
waitressing part-time. Your friend is of Mexican
descent and knows Spanish, so they break into a
warm, fluent conversation. Her Spanish is rapid-fire
authentic, while she's wearing a kimono and has
those Japanese chopsticks, or whatever they are,
pinned into her authentic, beautiful Asian hair. And
you think, this is pretty cool.

156
words

Lost

It takes a minute to get lost in the woods. You leave
the trail to find nature's men's room around some
tree, and when you bushwhack back to the trail, it's
not there. You're turned around. Suddenly there's
nothing but trees and brambles. Spiders and ticks.
Coyotes, foxes, feral dogs, a rumored cougar that
was sighted in Libertyville recently, holed-up bank
robbers, big-eyed owls, crowds of crows and vultures,
all watching. And you have to find the trail! You go
left and it's not there. Then right, but you're running
deeper in the woods. And you're not even in the Wild
West or Michigan; it's a Chicago forest preserve!
Cars are heard in the distance over your pounding
heart. So you run, knowing you'll eventually get out
of the woods, unless you wrongly run in a circle.
Then you'll never get out, and you run faster, crazed.
All in the time it takes to read this.

146
words

Relativity

Einstein's relativity theory has never been adequately explained, but we don't like to admit this. There are volumes popularizing it, the latest being Brian Greene's best-selling "The Fabric of the Cosmos," which just reviews relativity in the opening chapters before going on to meatier matters like quantum, super-string, multi-dimensional and theory-of-everything theories, by which time any honest reader must honestly admit he's lost and frankly didn't even understand the glossed over Einstein thing, yet alone the other stuff. So we'll take a minute to explain relativity: A minute spent eating pizza or watching certain cable channels with the sound off takes just under a minute, while a minute spent at a crafts & antiques fair that your wife dragged you to takes a warped hour and a half. Such is the space-time continuum or conundrum or whatever. This minute's up and it only took 40 seconds.

160
words

A Line Crossed

Some minutes evaporate into nothingness and are
never thought of again. Others stay with you. Like
the minute you first got to first base. Or the one
and only time you dunked a basketball. Or won
the trifecta. Maybe it's the minute you first tasted
deep dish pizza, with the cheese all gummy and
incredible. Or there's this minute: You and your
buddy and your girlfriend go into a crowded bar on
Lincoln Avenue. A drunk tells a joke to you and your
girl. He jabs his finger into her to emphasize the
punch line. You smile politely and your girl laughs
just to be polite. Suddenly your buddy pushes the
guy, knocks him down. It all happens so fast, this
minute. The drunk scurries out before you fully
understand what just happened. And your buddy
says, "Don't let some guy touch your girl's chest like
that." Your girl looks embarrassed. And you still are,
today, a million minutes later.

160
words

Better Path

Sometimes it takes a minute to make a friend or an enemy, and it could go either way. Example. You go into a men's room at a restaurant. There's this big guy changing his kid's diaper on the sink, and he's taking up most of the room there. The kid's all spread out and it's not pleasant. The atmosphere's even worse than usual in the men's room. Plus, you can't really get at the sink. This is the deciding moment. You want to give the guy a dirty look in the mirror, say something like "cheeez!" and leave in a huff. But something stops you, and you take another path. You say to the guy, "Ah, the joys of fatherhood." And you smile at him in the mirror as he struggles. He looks up and says, "Tell me about it." And he smiles. For a minute you both feel good instead of bad. A minute well spent. Like this one.

160
words

Fugu

Speaking of minutes, what if you had a minute to live? And what if you were in this time-sucking dilemma because you got fancy in a gourmet restaurant and ordered a rare (meaning uncommon) fish called fugu. This is a Japanese delicacy. Only a few chefs are trained to serve it. Only a few guys are rich enough to order it at $100 a serving. And nutty enough to eat it. (C'mon, does fish ever taste really good, even at the best of times?) Most fugu flesh is benign, but some contains poison that'll kill you in the time it takes to read this. The trick is to get just enough of the neurotoxin to feel a tingling in your lips, but no major paralysis, which could spoil your day by making it your last. Still, every year, 100 gourmands either overdo the fugu or go to a chef who's off his game. And their minute's up. More next time.

160
words

Warned

For a minute there, the hottest TV show not seen by the mass audience who doesn't get HBO, was "Curb Your Enthusiasm," starring Seinfeld co-creator Larry David. Why? Well, the show started out nicely a few years ago. Small audience. No fanfare. Offbeat, homemade look. A quirky cast who adlibbed, and looked like they liked each other off-camera. Funny stories. Then the show got discovered. Popularity kicked in, and Larry David revved it up a notch. His performance got hyper. The latest flight of shows, which had its final episode March 14, was eagerly anticipated by enthusiastic old fans and new ones too. Larry went over the top, and the show lost some magic. Should we be disappointed? Sure. Should we be surprised? No. After all, we'd been warned not to become enthusiastic about the show, hadn't we? All we had to do was pay heed to Larry David when he named it. He knew. Minute's up. More next time.

143
words

About the Author

Is this really necessary? Everything anybody could want to know about the author is evident in the minute-long rants, ravings, insights, experiences and stories in this book, since they're all true and reflect who this author is. But anyway, real quick: Former Creative Director of the Chicago office of a multi-national ad agency, founder/owner of a mid-sized Chicago ad agency. (Actually, not exactly mid-sized. Smallish, really. But big of heart). Writer of fiction and non-fiction published in national magazines, from the literary to the glossy, some in Australia and the U.K., creator and writer of the online magazine "Two-Fisted Birdwatcher," where more minute-like prose can be found, in case anyone wants more. The author lives in the Chicago area. He's a husband, father, grandfather with a Peter Pan complex, and could've played pro basketball if he were only a little taller.

143
words

Acknowledgements

The Got A Minute column from which this book's selections are taken ran on The Guy Page in the Sunday Chicago Tribune's "Q" section from 2004 through 2008. "Q" was for quality of life; the section had variety and fun, rather than news stories, typical Sunday stuff. The Tribune editor who recognized the value in short word counts deserves recognition himself, Ross Werland. Thanks, Ross. (How's that for a short word count.) And thanks also to my writer friend Marc Davis, who knew Ross, and got us together journalistically. But none of this would have ever happened if a cute girl I met in college hadn't said she only dated creative guys. So, back then, I started writing to impress her, and she was very encouraging. My wife still is, and without her proofreading and all-around good judgment, this book wouldn't have happened.